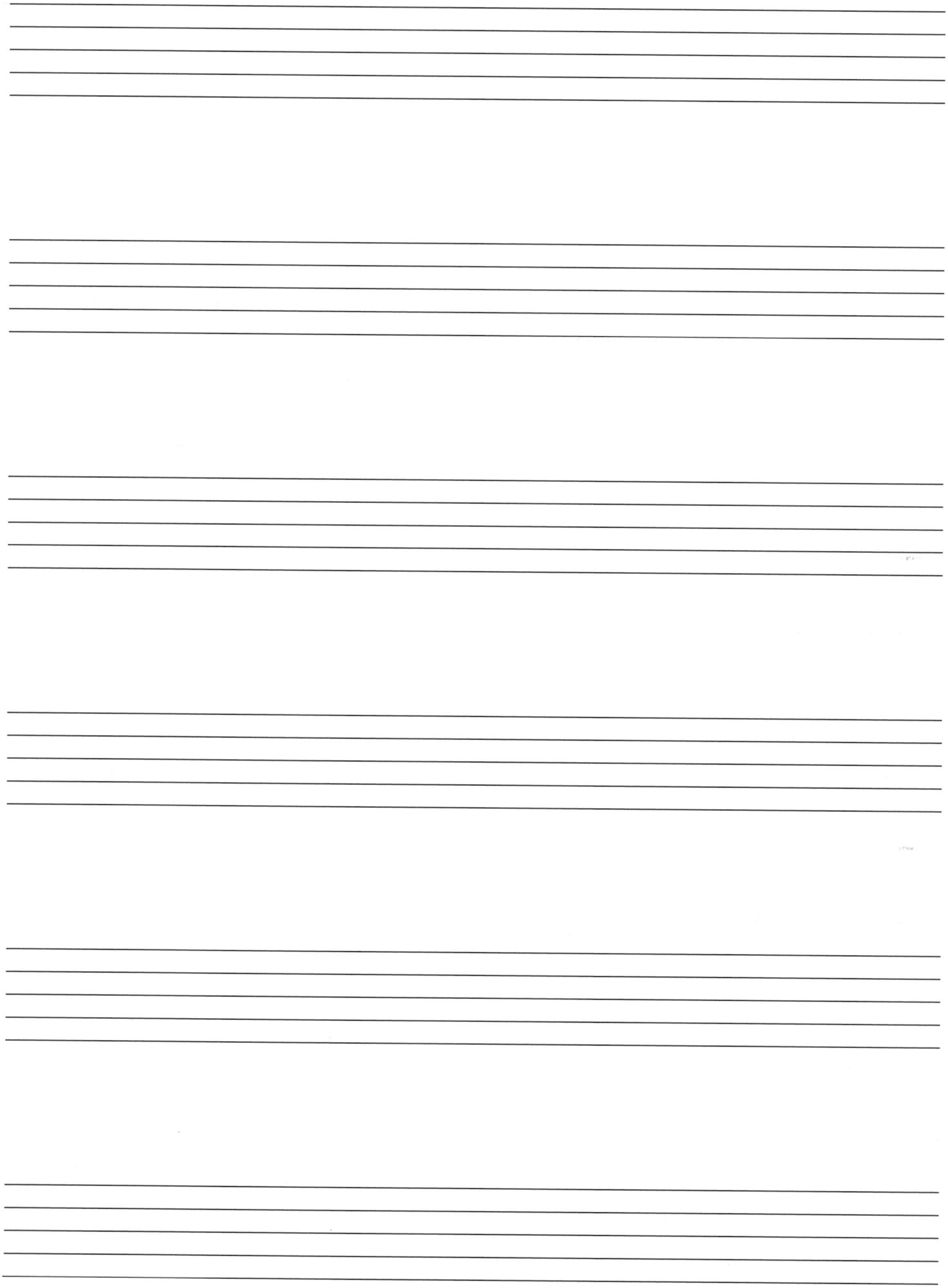

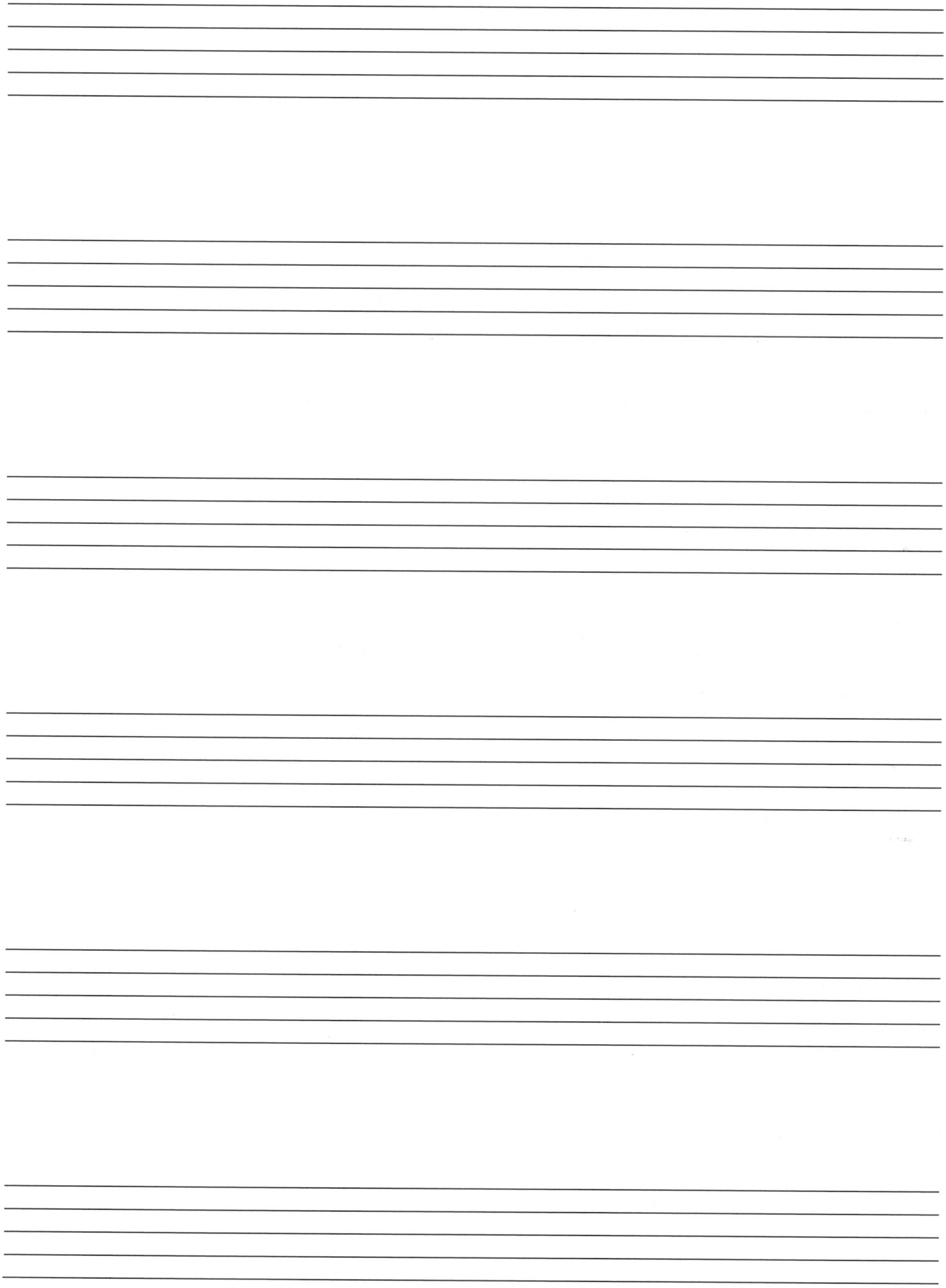

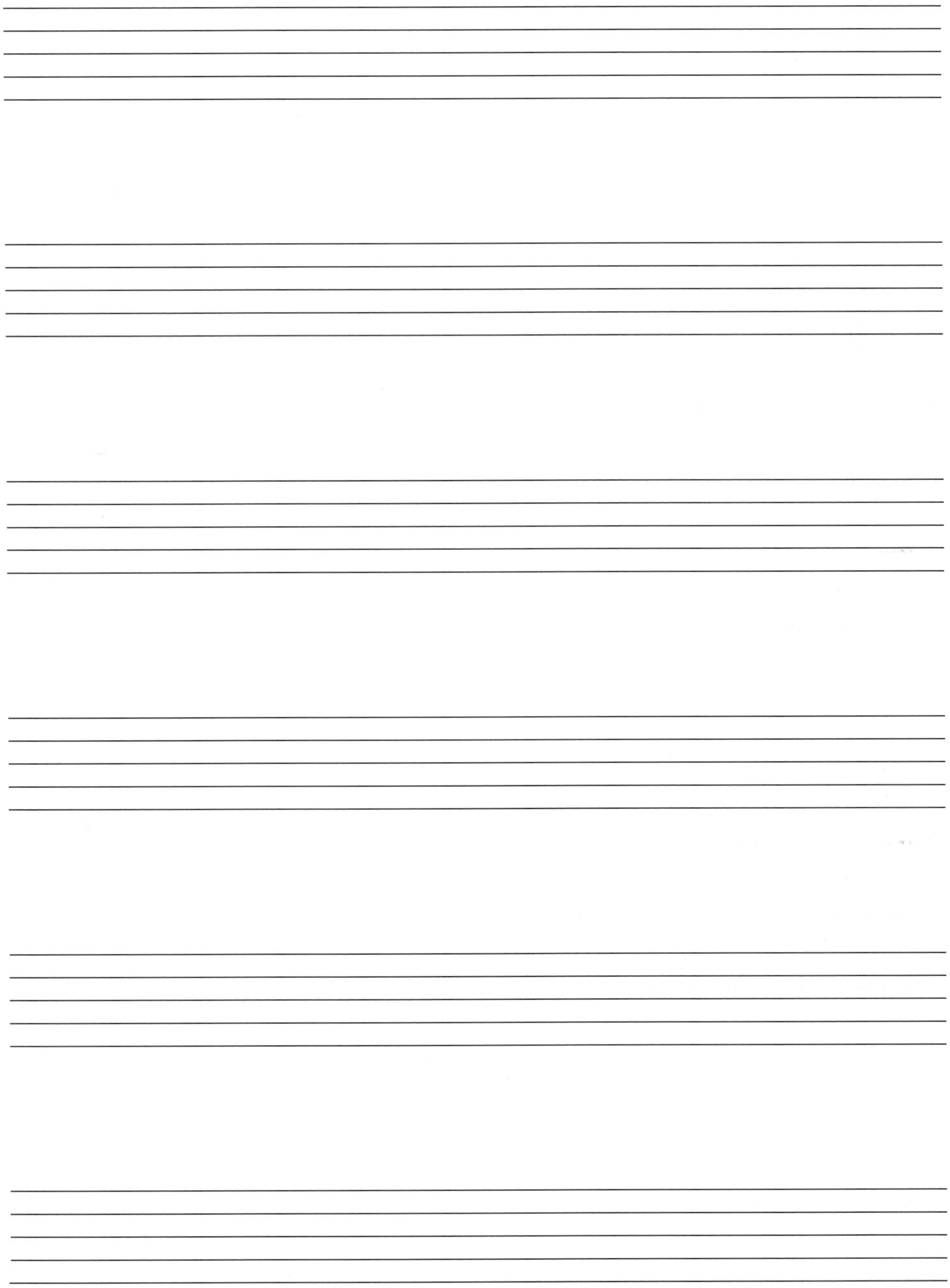

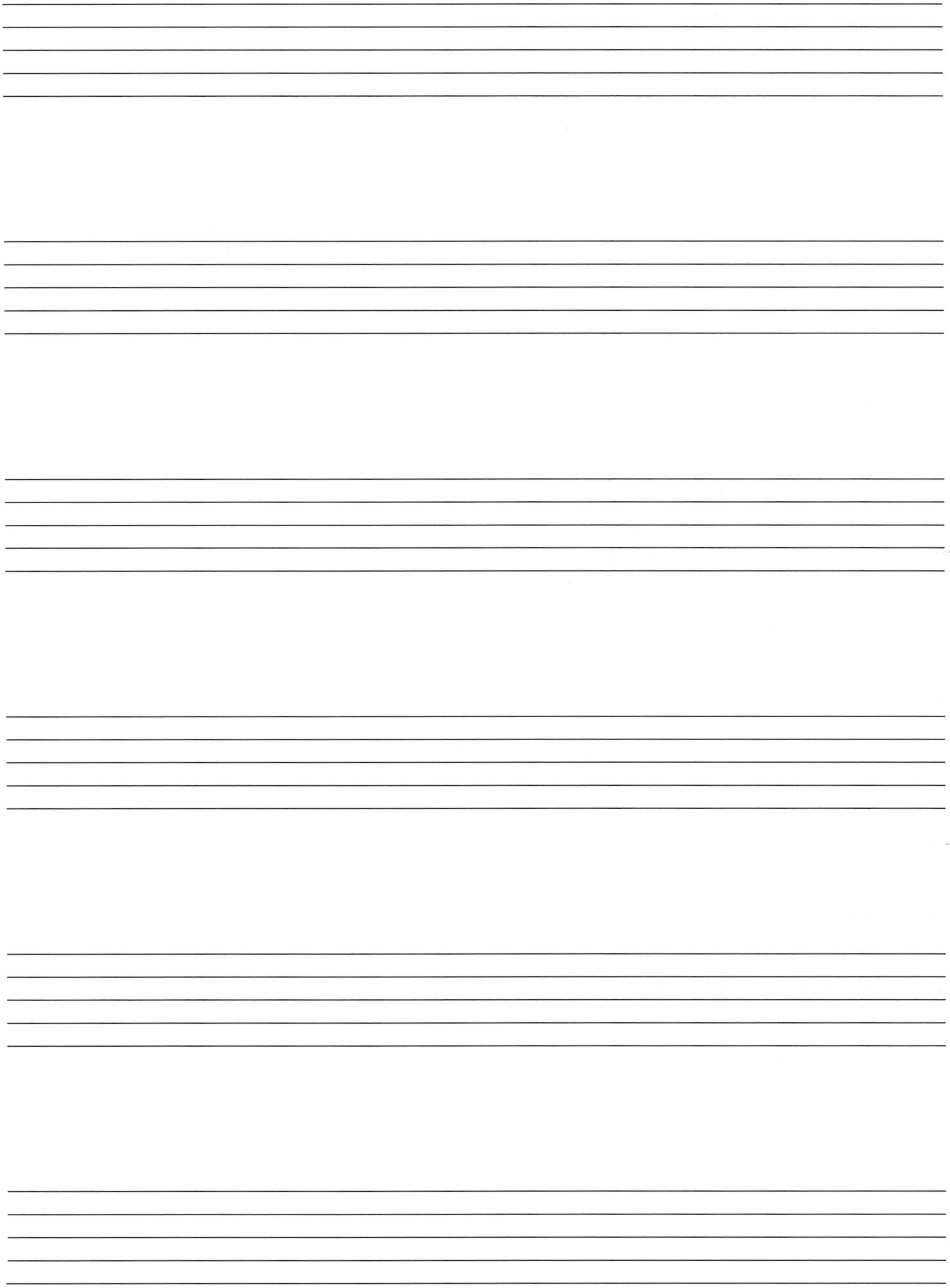

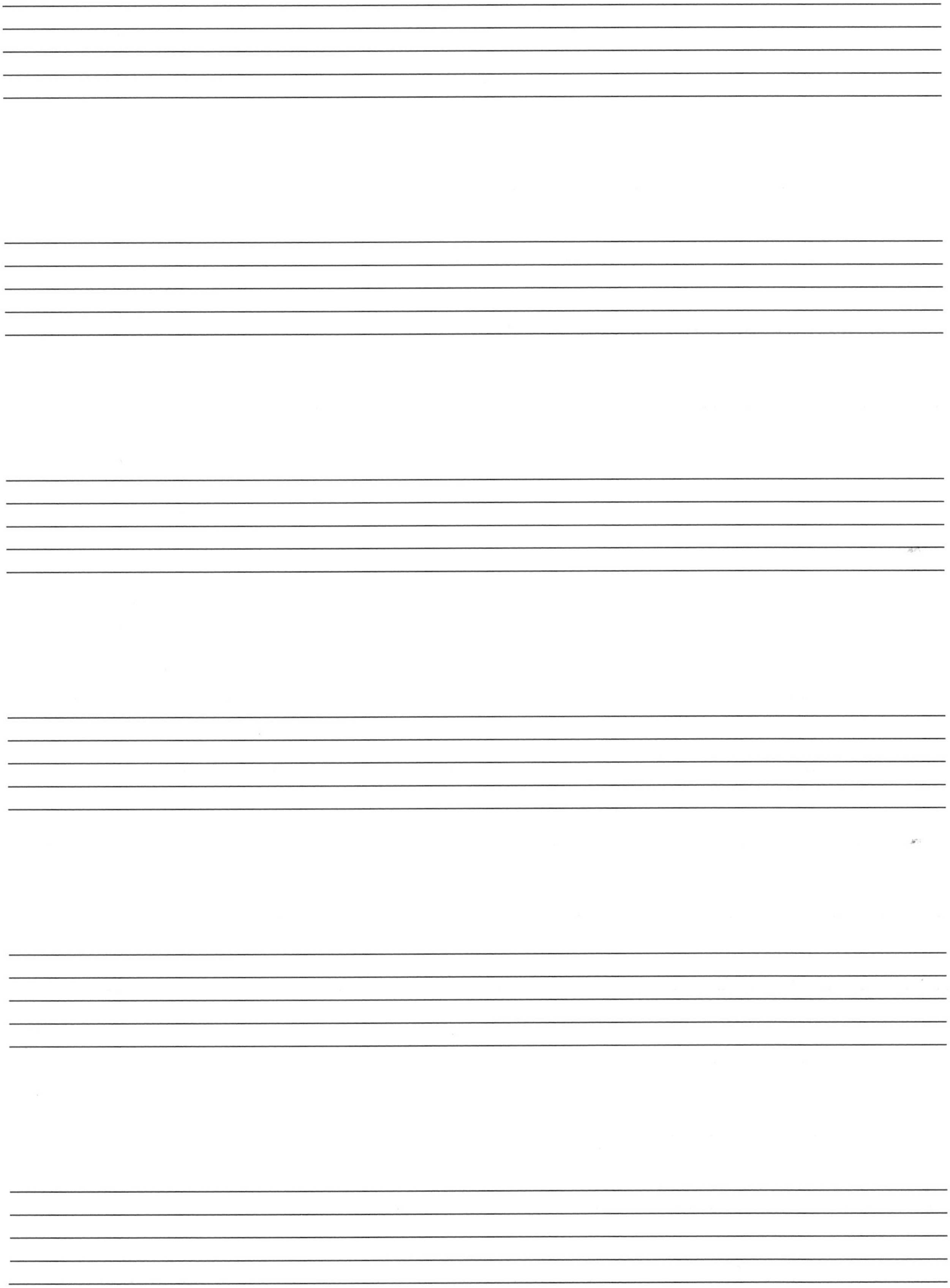

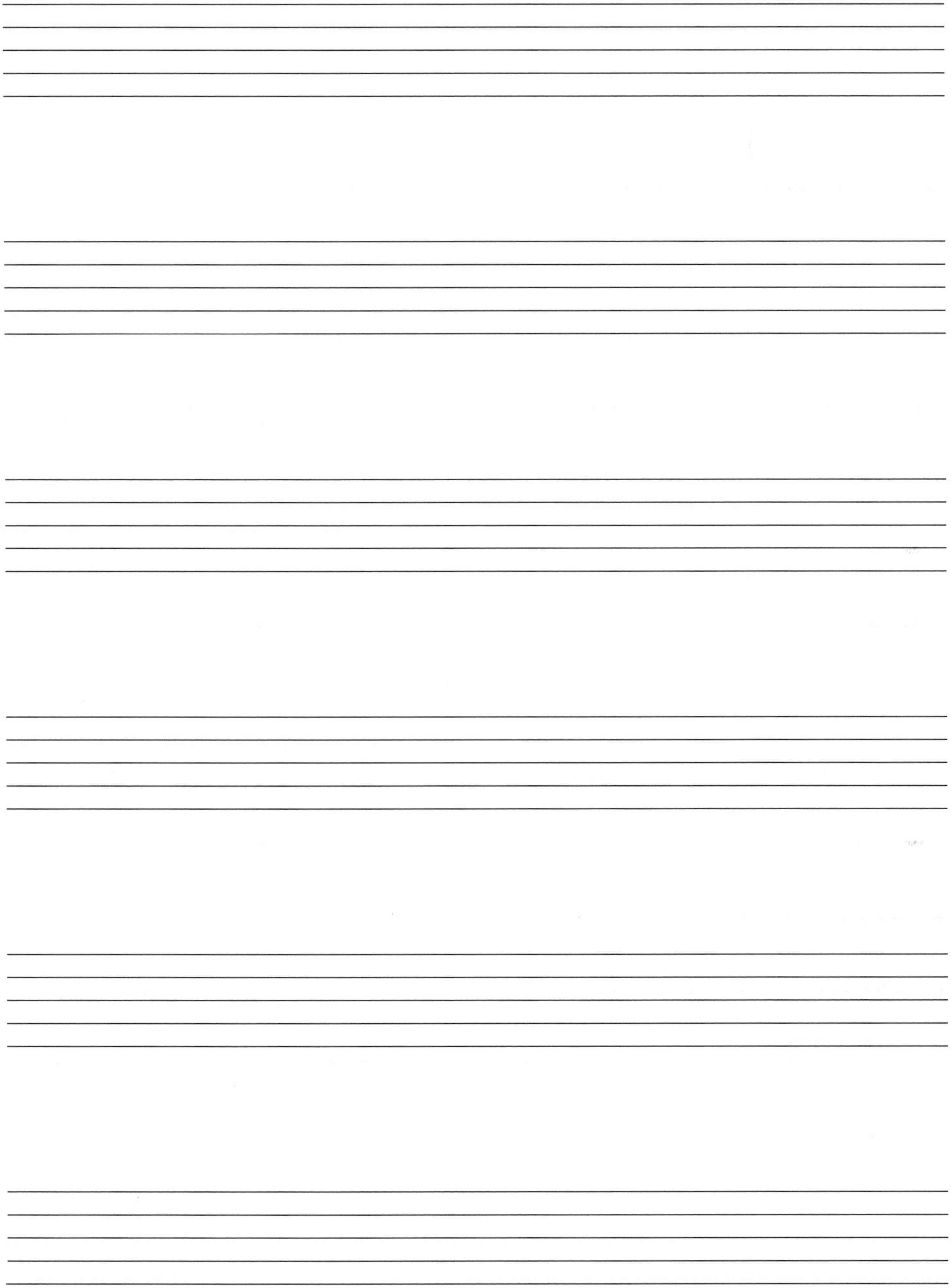

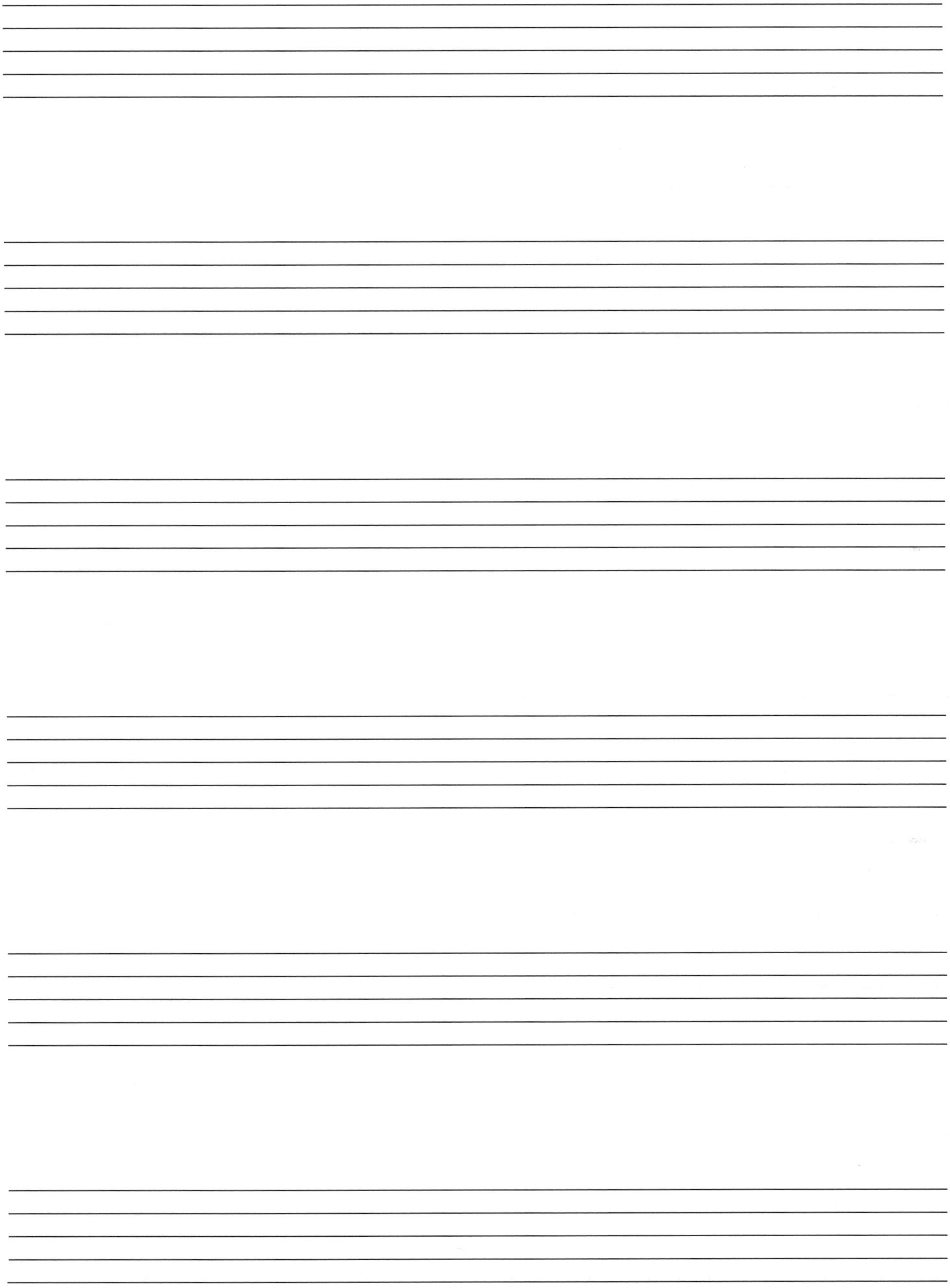

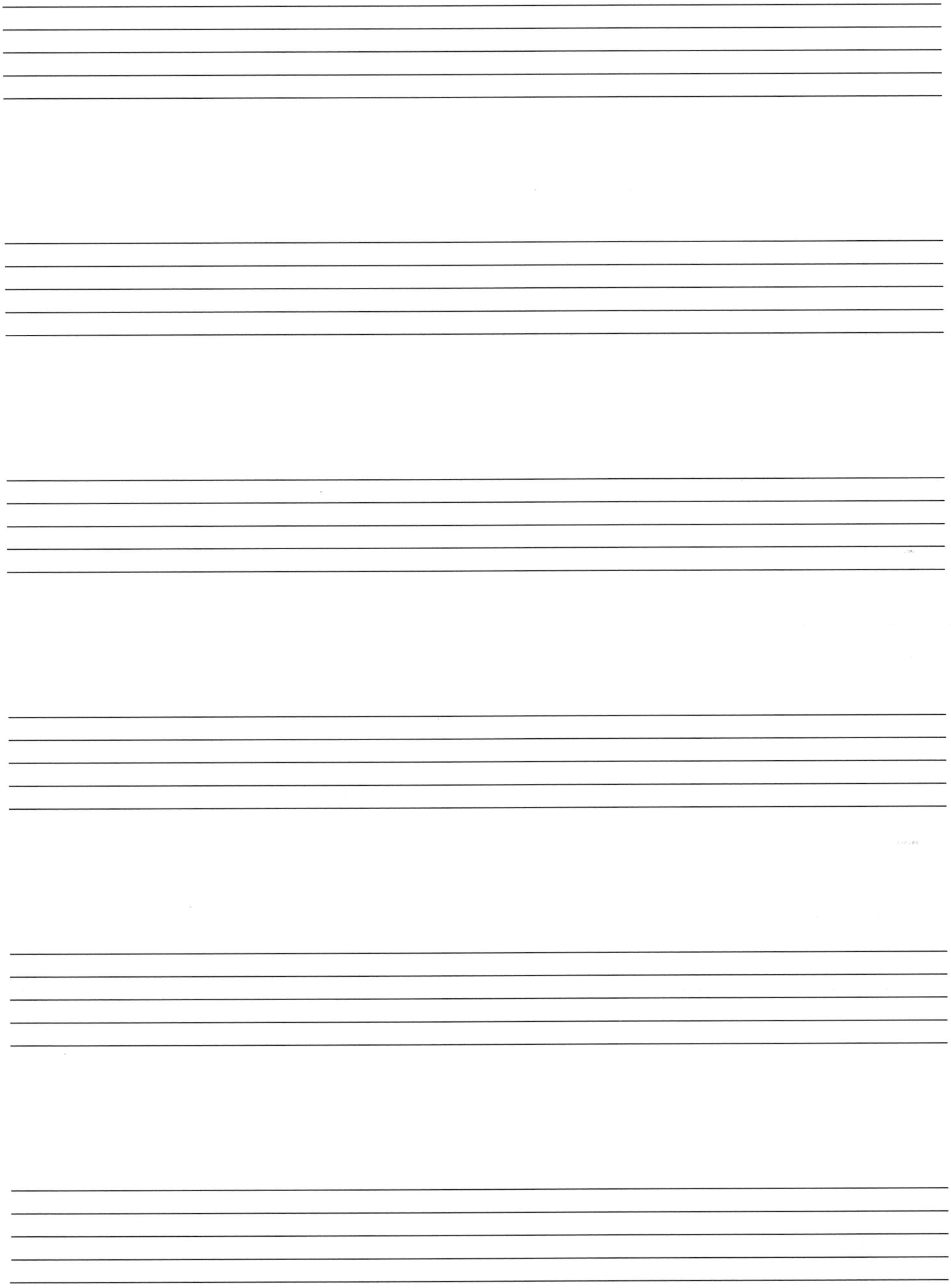

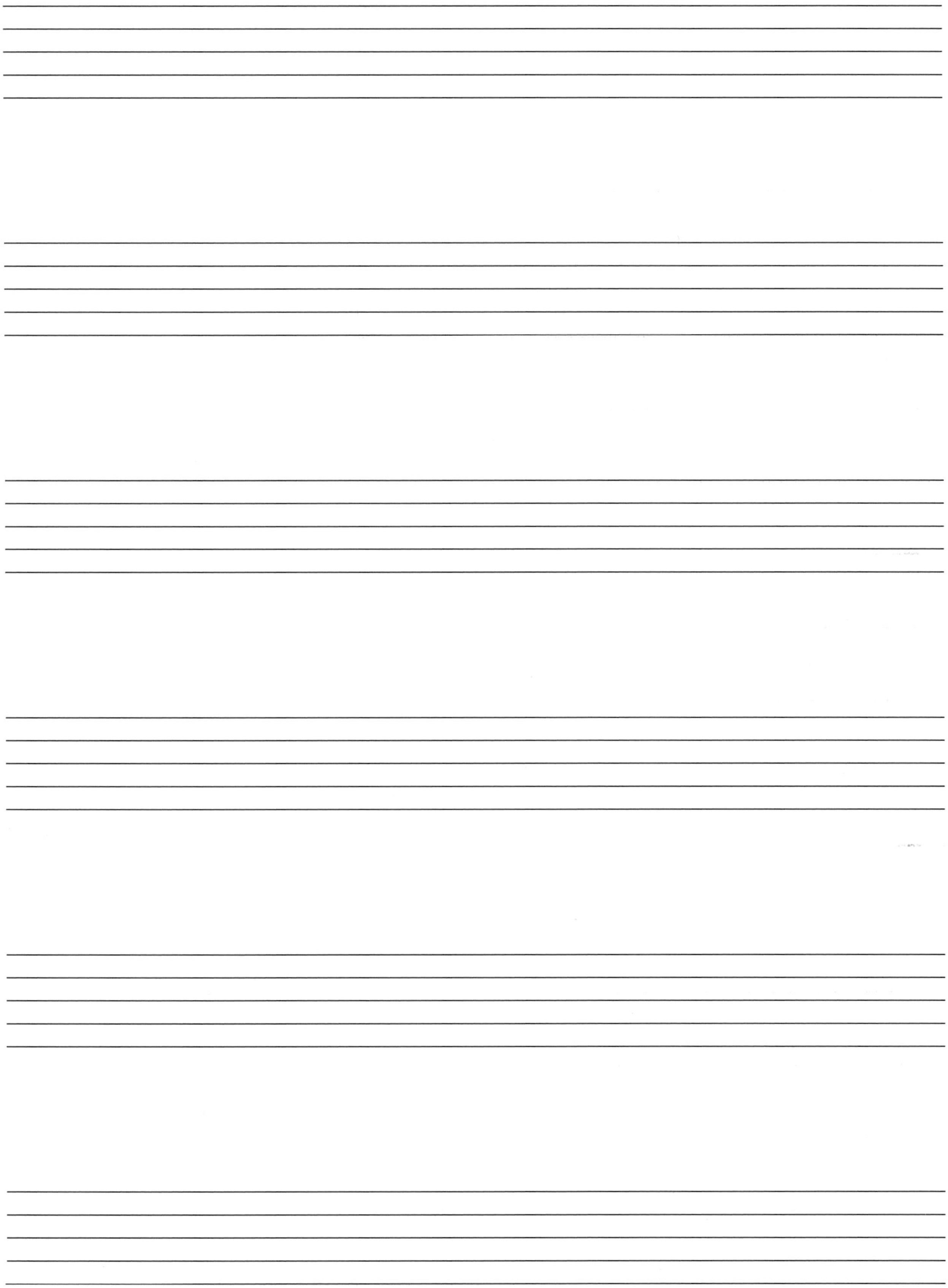

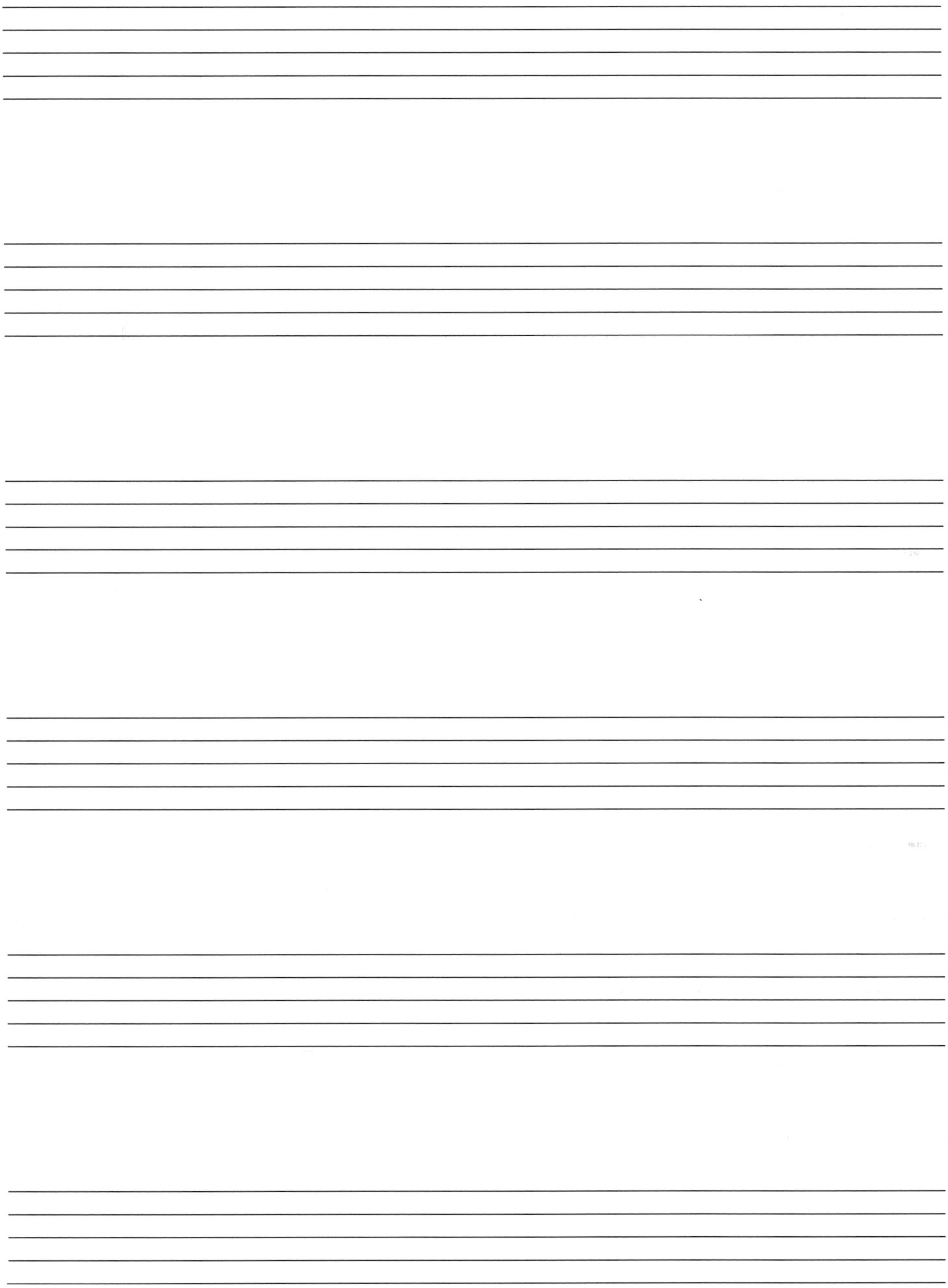

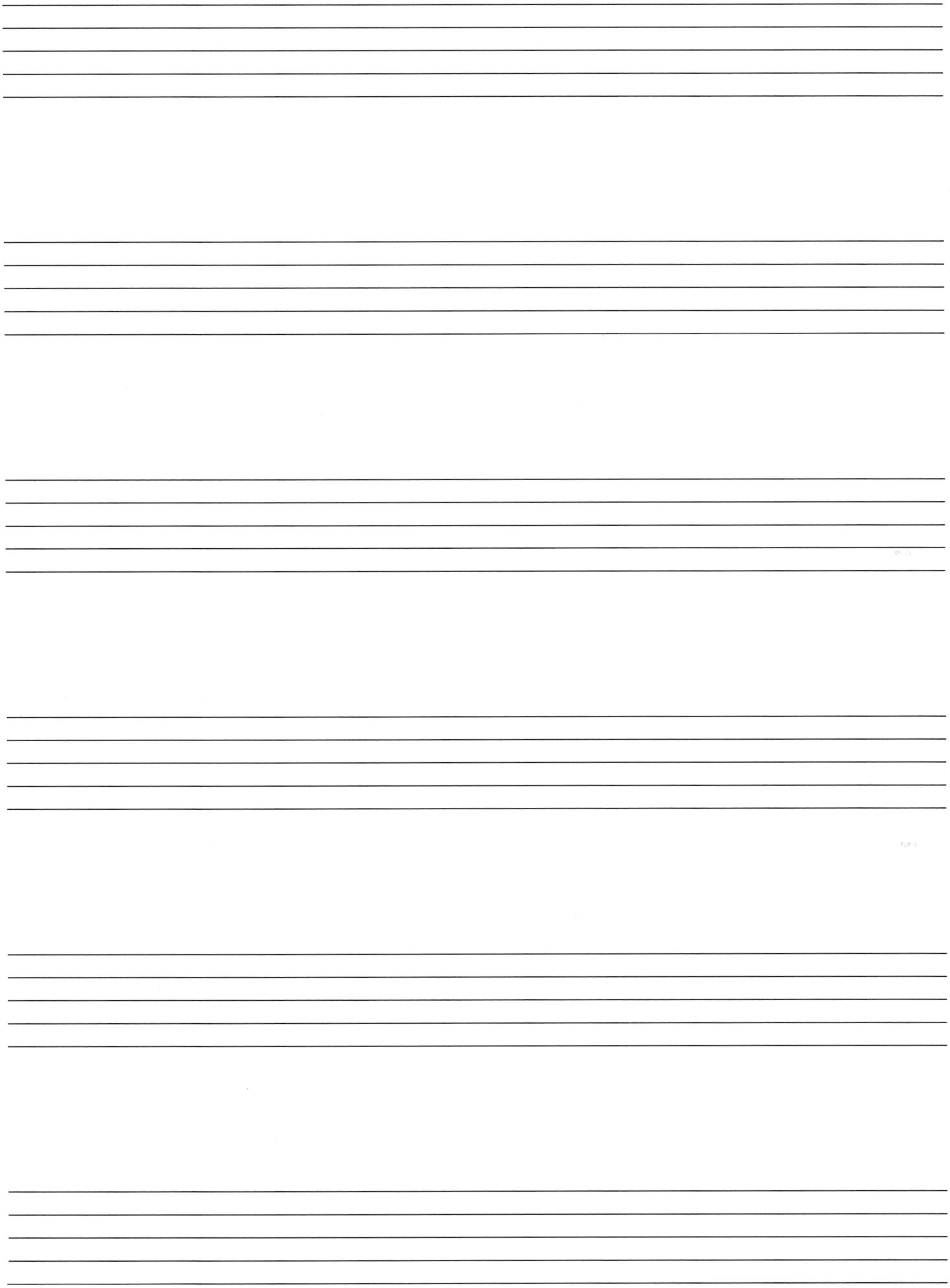

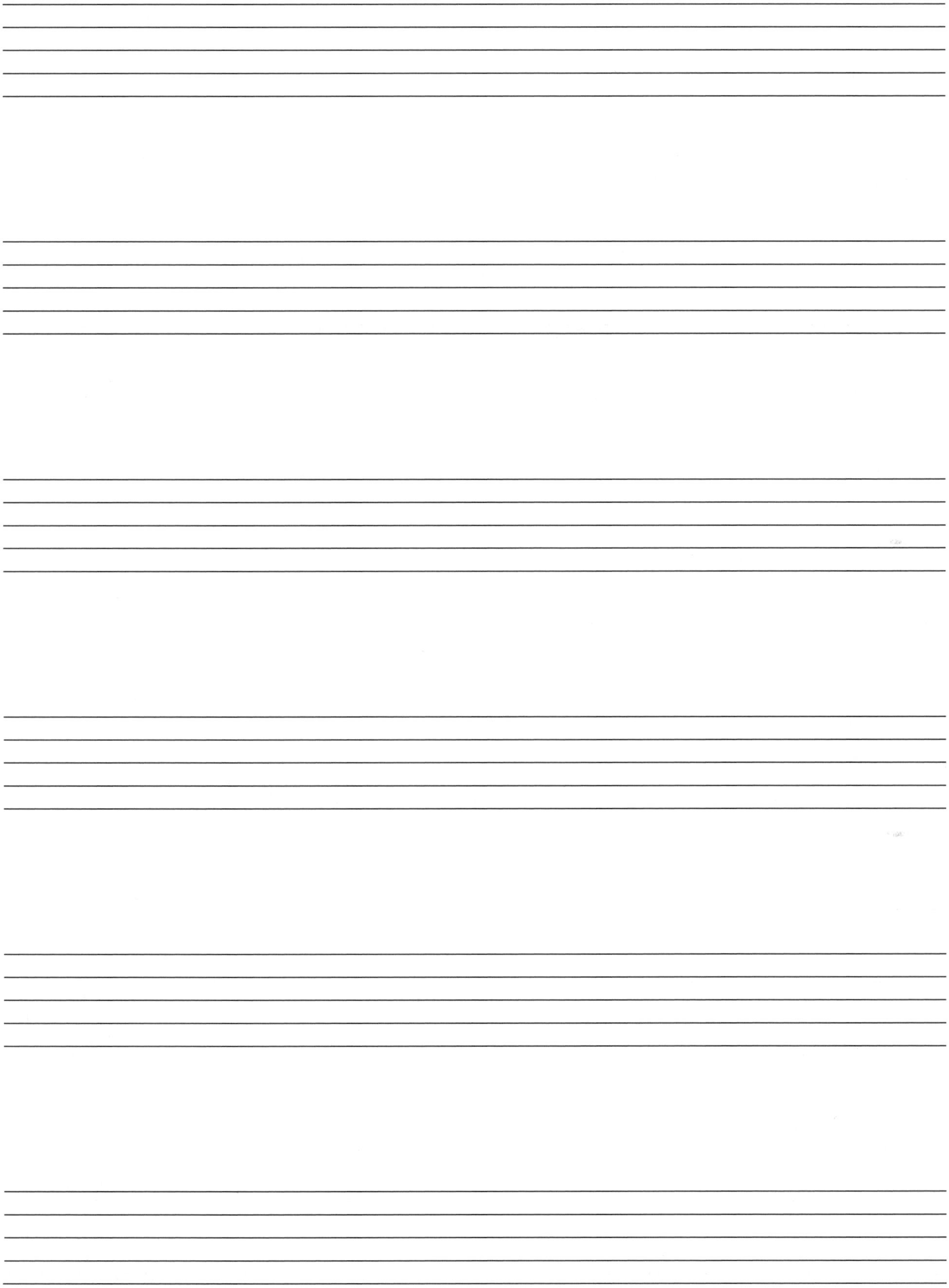

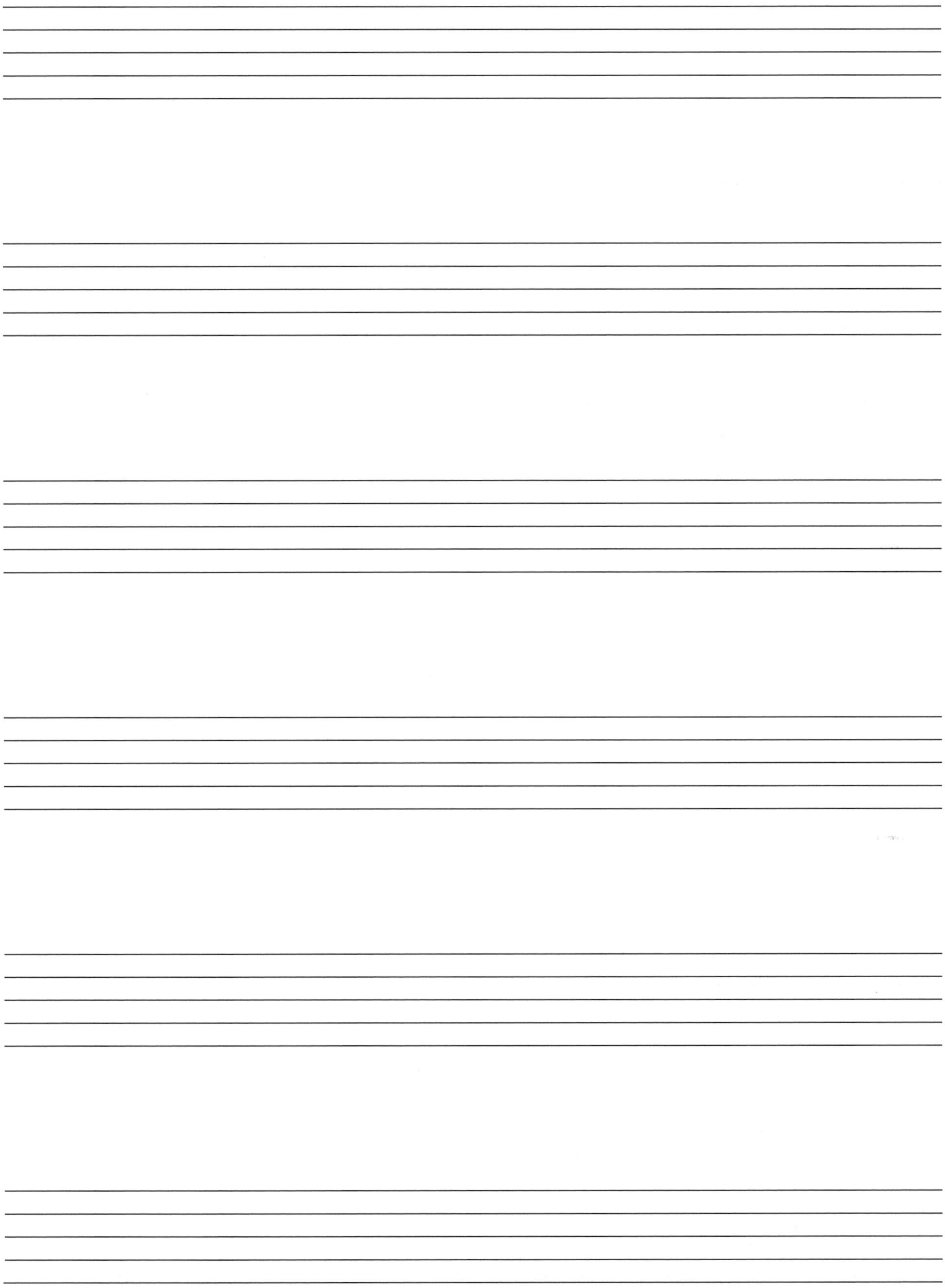

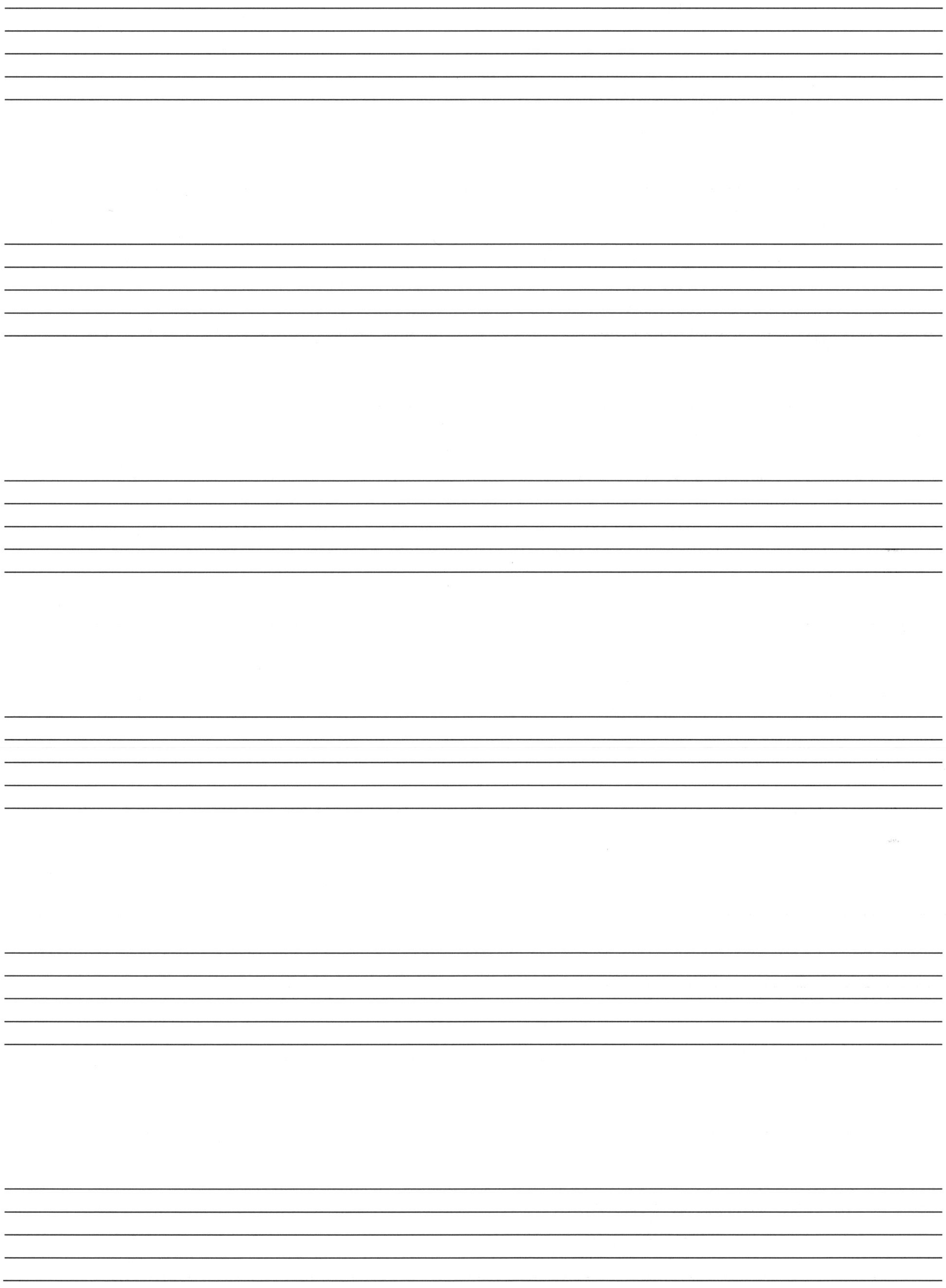

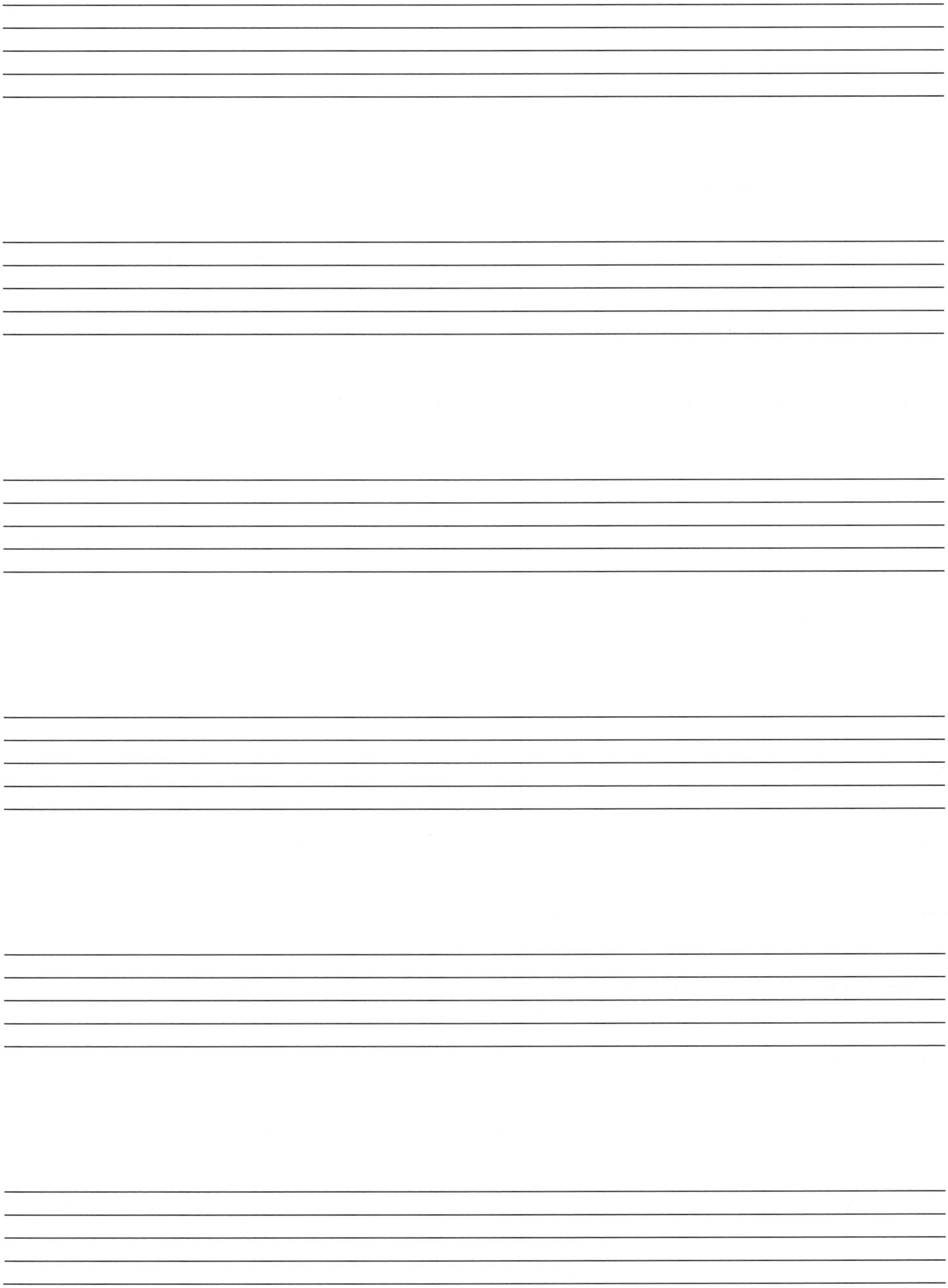

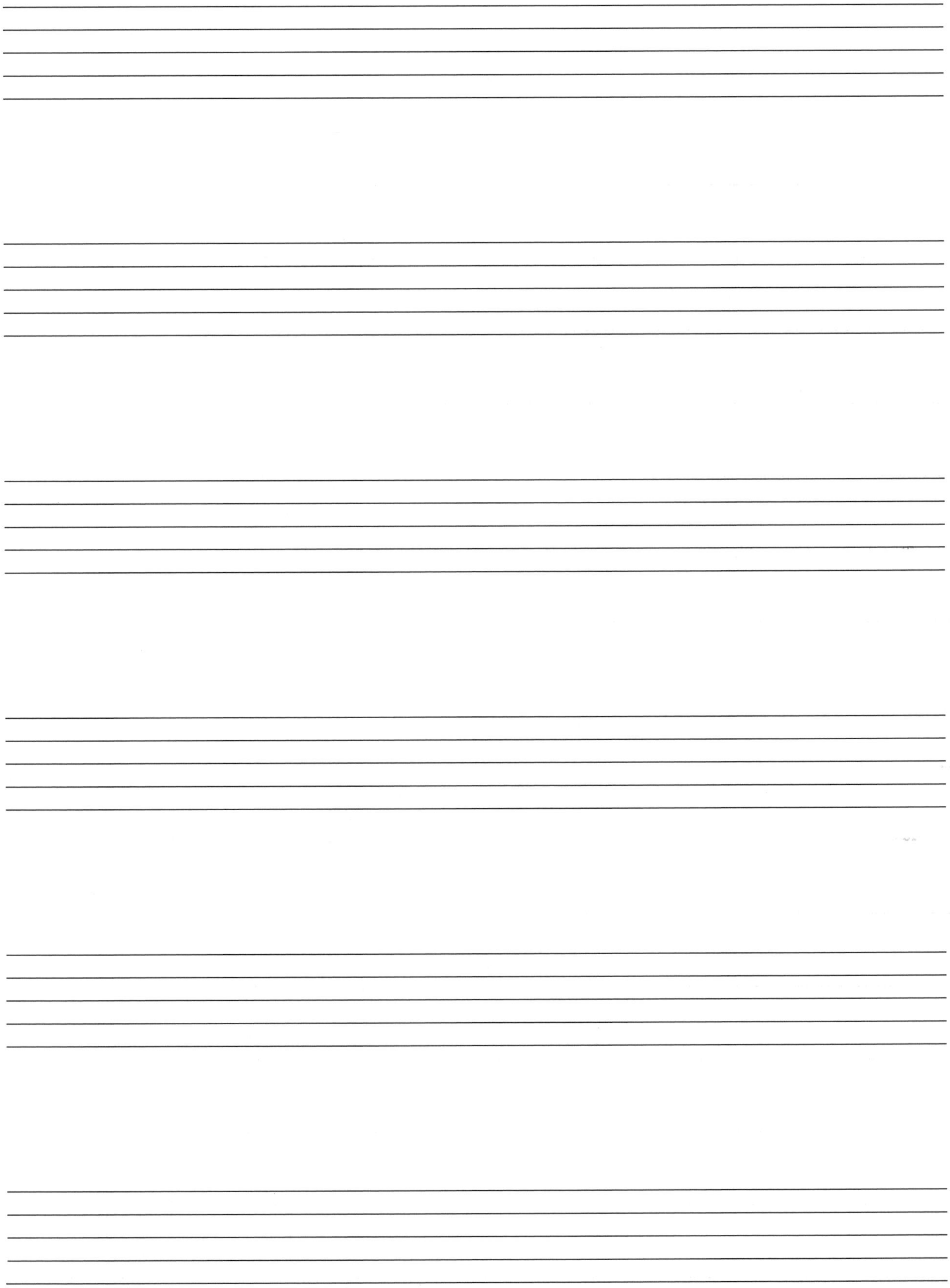

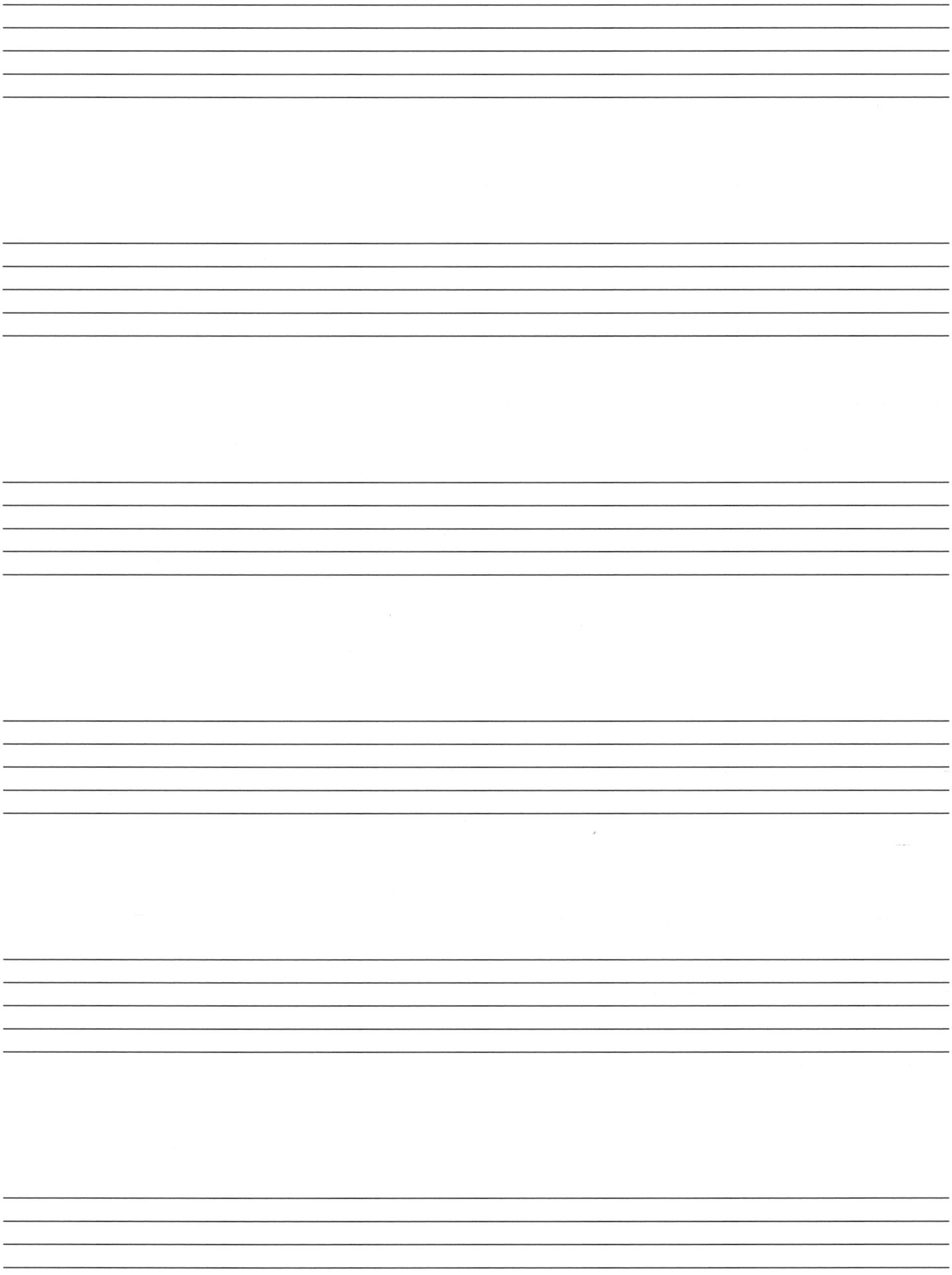

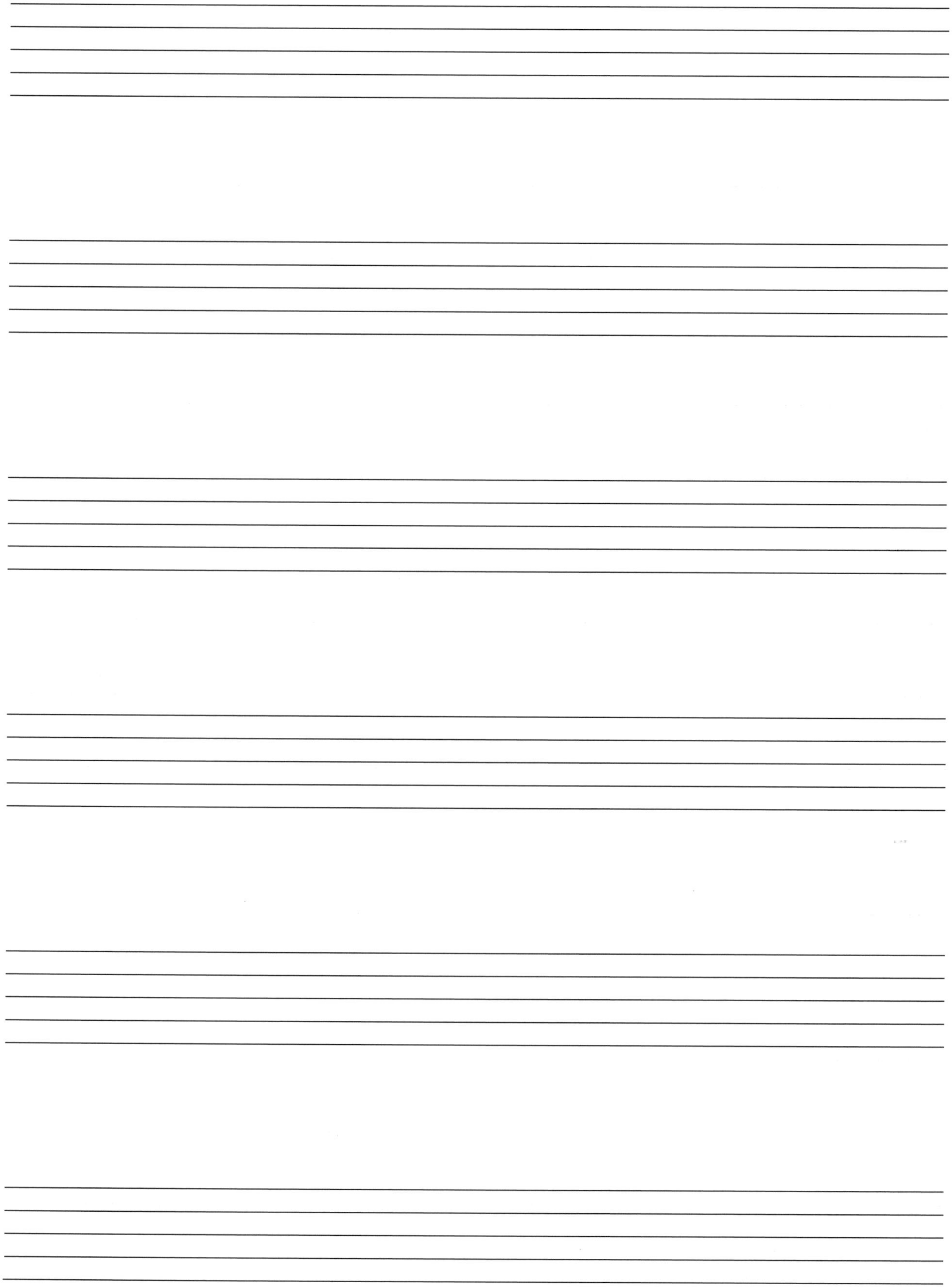

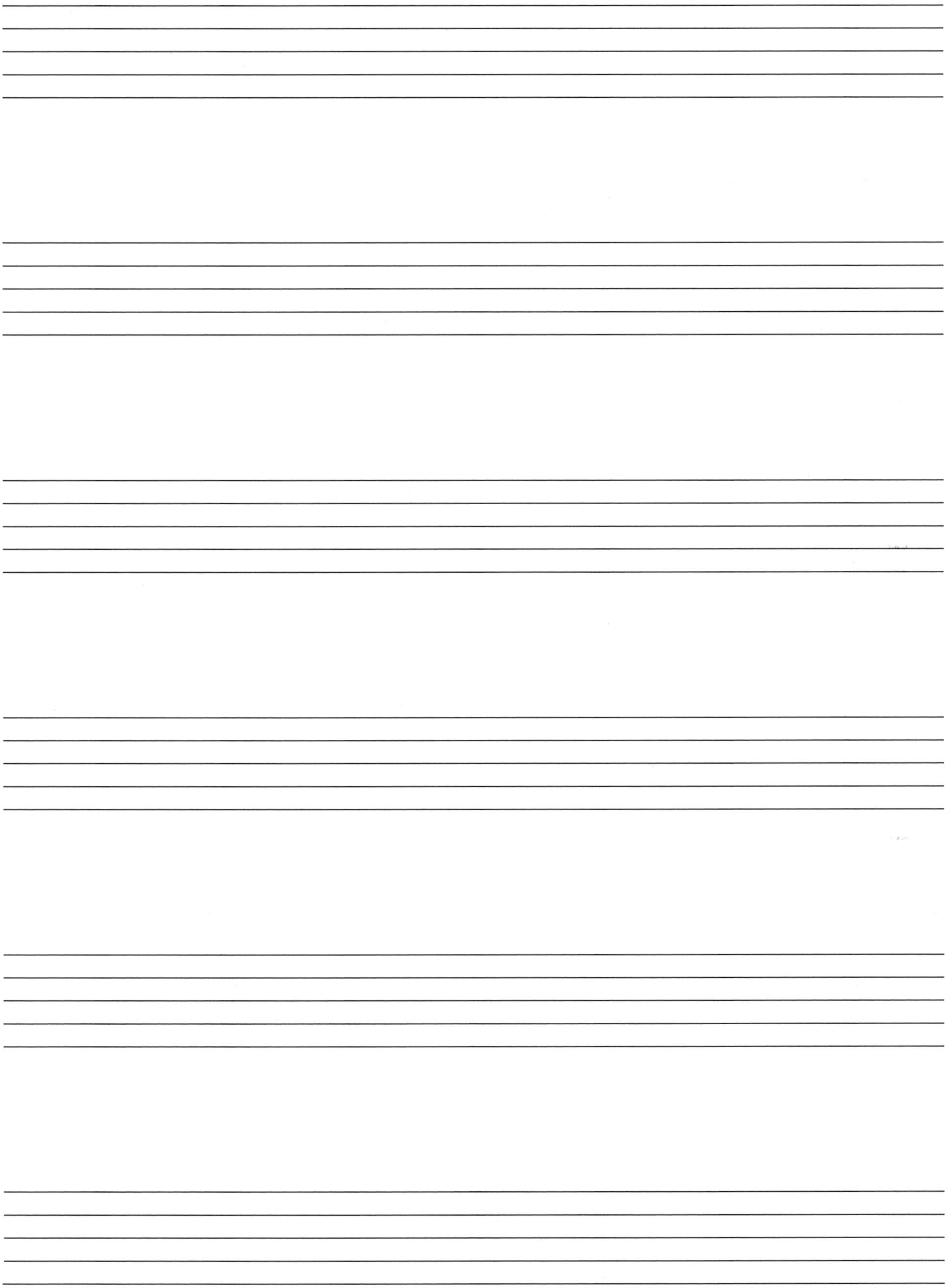

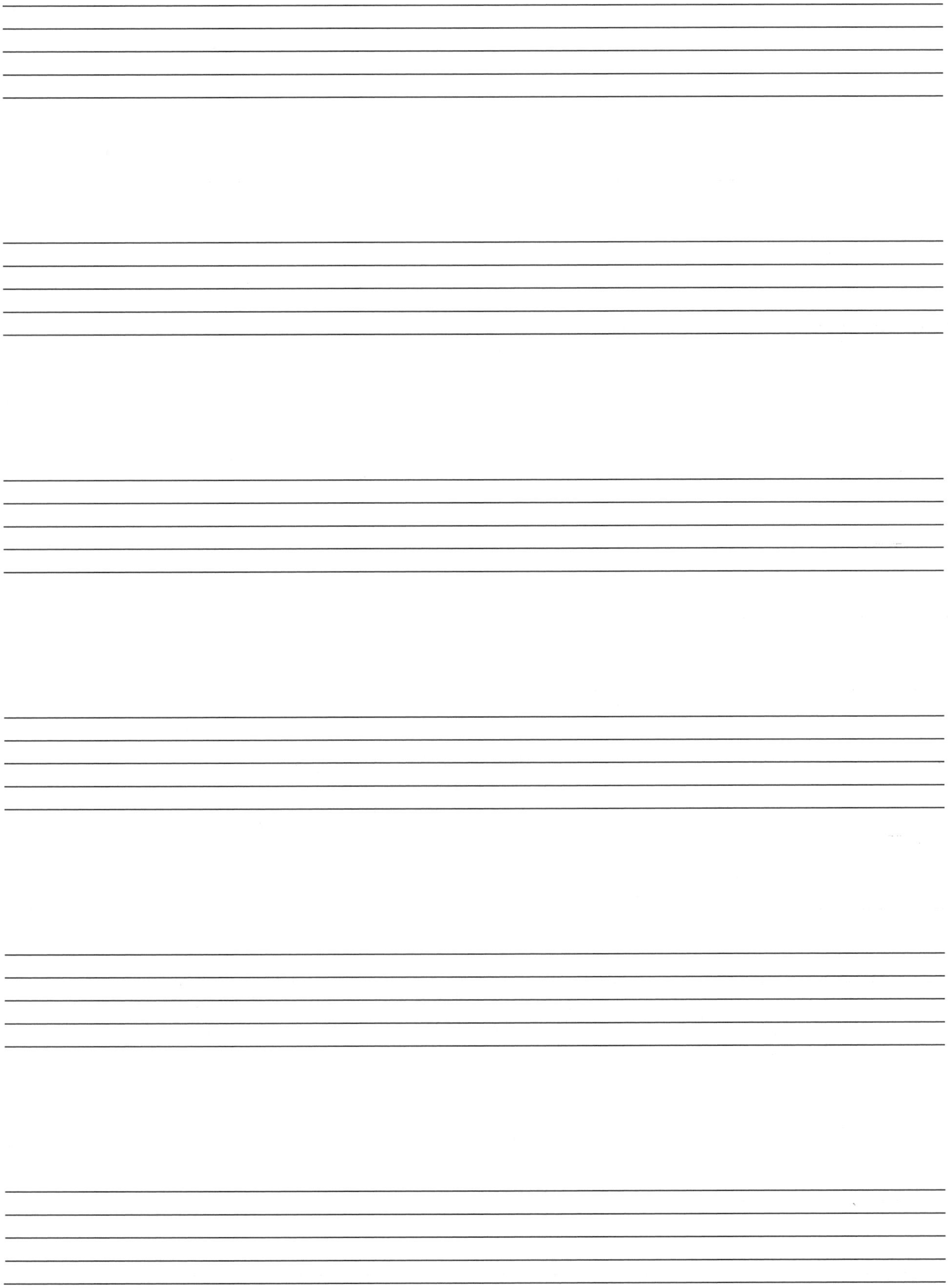

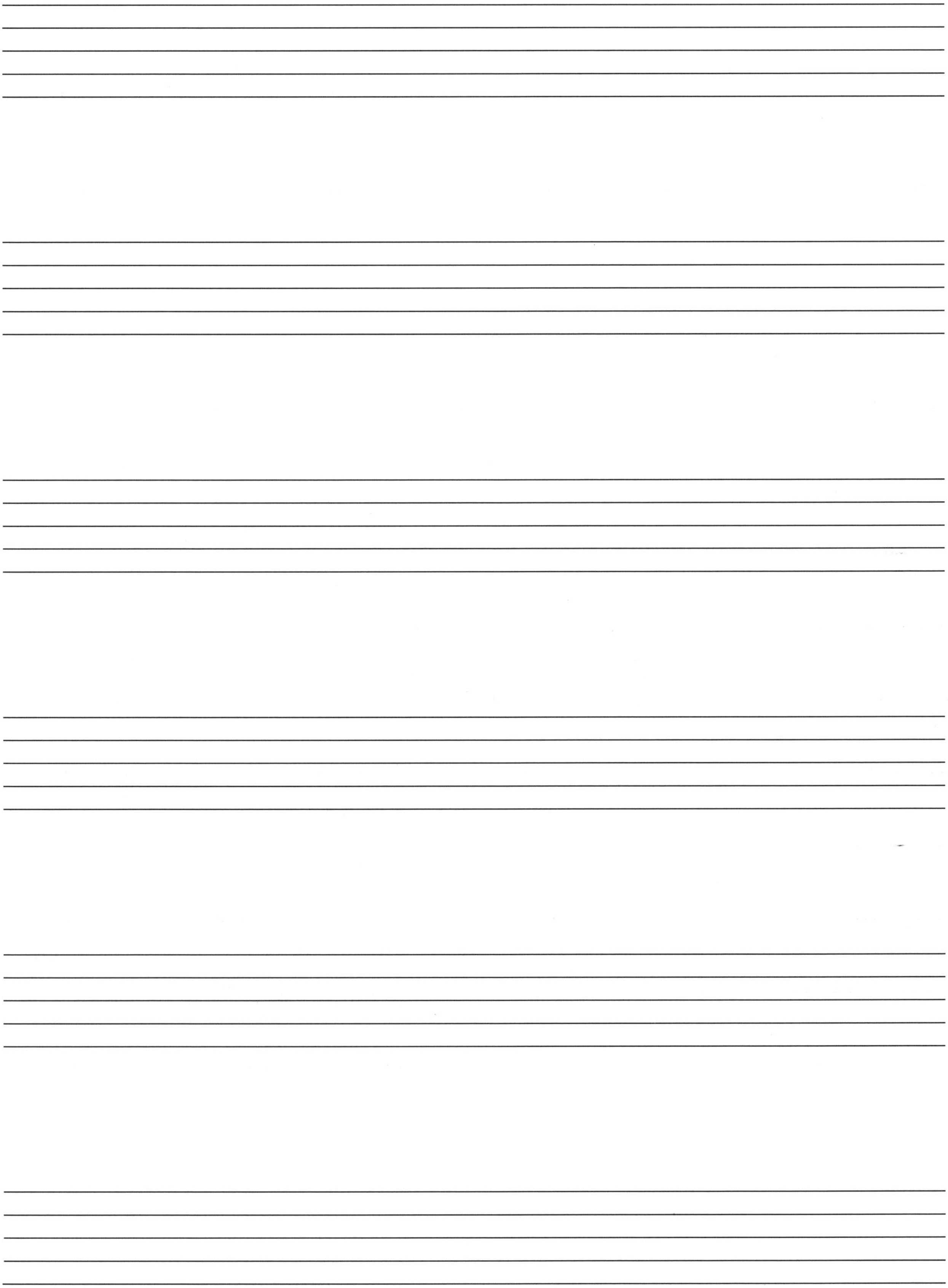

Made in United States
Orlando, FL
08 March 2022

15527067R00057